REMEMBER YESTERDAY

*A
Century
of
Photographs*

Pierre Berton

Remember Yesterday

A CENTURY OF PHOTOGRAPHS

The Canadian Centennial Library

≪

THE
CANADIAN CENTENNIAL
LIBRARY

WEEKEND
MAGAZINE

McCLELLAND
AND STEWART
LIMITED

≪

Pierre Berton, *Editor-in-chief*
Frank Newfeld, *Art Director*
Ken Lefolii, *Managing Editor*

THE
CANADIAN CENTENNIAL
PUBLISHING CO. LTD.,
150 Simcoe St., Toronto, Canada

Contents

The Pictures In This Book

are designed as a kind of visual essay on the social development of the nation in the first century of its existence. It is in no sense definitive, since these photographs have been winnowed down from an original selection of about ten thousand. Nor are they necessarily the best pictures from an artistic or photographic point of view. They have been chosen with another purpose in mind: to try to show, in as lively and entertaining a manner as possible, how ordinary and generally anonymous Canadians have lived and struggled, toiled and disported themselves over the past hundred years. There has been little attempt to chronicle specific political or national events save when they have reflected something of the everyday way of life in their times. What I have been interested in chiefly has been the *look* of the people and the *look* of the country during those decades which are invariably referred to in retrospect as "the good old days."

In a sense, then, this is a book of trends. There are sod huts and skyscrapers here, saloons and coffee houses, bobsleds and Bennett buggies. It is also a book of styles, liberally sprinkled with bustles and shirtwaists, mutton-chop whiskers and bobbed hair, high-button shoes, bikinis, cloche hats and handlebar moustaches. Finally, it is a book of fads, from the great bicycle craze of the 1890s through the bathing-beauty contests of the 1920s to the beatnik era of the late 1950s. And if from the ocean of unidentifiable Canadian faces, New and Old, a familiar one now and then emerges

Toronto's first photographer, Eli J. Palmer, made this carte de visite *in 1863. The subject is* Globe *publisher George Brown.*

–a politicking John A. Macdonald, a globe-trotting Gordon Sinclair, a wartime Johnny Wayne– it is for no other reason than that these people were also part of the fads and fancies of their time. Their faces are a kind of recognizable trademark stamped on their own decades.

The greatest fad of all, of course, has been the lasting one that makes this book possible. From tintype to candid, from Kodak to Polaroid, photography in all its forms has never ceased to fascinate the continent. The camera craze neatly spans the Canadian century. When Confederation dawned people were as obsessed with stereoscopes as they later became with 3-D; and another new fad, spawned by the camera, had all but taken over the nation: its very name, "family album," conjures up memories of Victorian parlours, bustled matrons and unsmiling, whiskered patriarchs.

What Canadian attic or closet does not contain today, within its dusty clutter, one of those original family albums? The best of them sold for fifty dollars (at a time when a dollar would buy four hearty dinners). They were so durable, with their heavily embossed covers, their thick leaves and their firm hinges, that a century of thumbing has failed to dent or tatter them. From these pages stare the stiff, starched faces of our ancestors–all of them–mamas, papas, grandparents and in-laws, not to mention platoons of uncles and aunts, phalanxes of cousins fifteen times removed and even casual family friends; for when the family album fad got going there was no stopping it. And each visage bears that fixed look of grim determination which every one of us would assume if told, not to watch the birdie, but to hold that pose for at least twenty seconds.

The photographs in these early albums are all of a size: two and one-eighth by three and one-half inches. These were the *cartes de visite* that Oliver Wendell Holmes called "the social currency, the sentimental greenbacks of civilization." To this day no other kind of photograph has exceeded the *carte* in popularity. Some were printed on paper from wet-plate negatives; some were tintypes. The very language was salted with photographic phrases: when a politician, asked if he would support Confederation, replied, "Not on your tintype," everybody knew what he meant.

By the year of Canada's birth, then, the photograph was a well-established social fixture. The early pictures in this book show that accomplished professionals were already at work in city and on frontier. As early as 1858 a Toronto photographer, Humphrey Lloyd Hime, had accompanied the Assiniboine and Saskatchewan Exploring Expedition surveying routes for settlement west of the Red River.

Hime must have been a man of considerable ability; among other achievements he stands as the only photographer ever to be elected president of the Toronto Stock Exchange. Besides his food and camping equipment he had to pack all the complicated photographic gear of those days–

An 1867 stereoscope: Presbyterian missionaries leave Halifax for New Zealand.

enormous camera, tripod, bales of chemicals and developing trays, portable darkroom and all—by canoe, dog cariole and Red River cart.

The paper photograph printed from a wet-plate negative was less than a decade old and, by modern standards, maddeningly cumbersome to make, especially outside a studio. Listen, for instance, to Harry Pollard, a pioneer Calgary photographer, recalling those wet-plate days:

"We'd get up at four in the morning. Even then we were pushed to get our plates coated and our printing paper made for the day. It was cold, dirty work in the winter. I'm always surprised by how many good pictures got made on the frontier. It wasn't just packing all that equipment along; as soon as you had an exposure you had to develop it or lose it." (The plates dried in an hour and were useless after that.) *"Every time you took a picture you had to set up your dark-room tent first. Nobody's ever worked at photography the way those boys did."*

In spite of such difficulties, Hime made some truly great photographs, thirty of which were later published in London in a portfolio about the Canadian west.

By the time of Confederation, the wet plate was securely established. Indeed, photography had come a long way in the twenty-eight years since the invention of the daguerreotype, or "the new art of sunpainting," as the Quebec *Gazette* called it when it heralded the discovery in 1839.

It is no accident that Louis Daguerre, the French painter, was also the co-inventor of the diorama. This contrivance produced intriguing optical effects by means of giant transparent paintings through which coloured light was admitted. Daguerre wanted to get his scenes on canvas without going to the trouble of painting them, and he hit upon the idea of using the sixteenth-century Italian *camera obscura*. This original camera was a small dark room with a shutter. When a pinpoint of light was admitted through the shutter onto a white screen in the room, the reverse image of whatever was outside the window appeared on the screen. The effect seemed almost magical. It did not take long to scale the room down to a small box with a convex lens for the light and a piece of ground glass for a screen; but until Daguerre came along, nobody had really figured out a way to make the reflection permanent.

Daguerre made use of a known principle: that various salts of silver (such as silver iodide) are sensitive to light and will change colour when exposed to light. He used a sheet of silver-plated copper, the surface of which he treated with iodine vapour. This plate was exposed in the camera for a number of minutes (sometimes as long as half an hour) and then developed with vapourized mercury. Finally, the image was fixed with hypo-sulfite of soda in much the same way that modern photographers fix their pictures. The chemical action produced highlights of mercury and shadows of silver on a mirror-like surface, giving a brilliance and clarity that has never been matched by modern paper photographs.

Royal Engineers of the International Boundary Survey preparing wet plates in 1873.

This early daguerreotype was made in 1850.

Daguerreotypes are easily damaged, but they do not fade. Some of them are as sharp and clear today as they were a century and more ago. No more permanent method of making a picture has ever been developed since this first one. But there were disadvantages: the picture, being reproduced on a metal mirror, could not be seen at all unless viewed from the right angle. It was always reversed, left to right, so that every man's hair was parted on the wrong side. Moreover, there was no way to make copies of it.

Everybody realized at once that a milestone in art had been reached. "Painting is dead from this day," one of Daguerre's artist contemporaries cried. In a sense he was right. Representational art began to die and a new abstract style to take its place—a style now being imitated by photographers, as the colour pictures on pages twenty-four and twenty-five demonstrate. From the very first, daguerreotype photographers were called "artists."

The remarkable thing about the new art is the speed with which it was perfected. All the really major advances (save for the Polaroid process, which came after World War II) were made in the first half century. Though Daguerre himself photographed only landscapes, others swiftly learned to cut the thirty-minute exposure time to sixty-five seconds by using larger lenses and shorter focal lengths. At the height of the daguerreotype craze in the 1850s there were more than three million photographs being turned out

Introduction

A popular ambrotype taken at Table Rock, Niagara Falls, about 1857.

annually in North America. By this time studio subjects didn't have to hold still for longer than half a minute. In sunlight the exposure time was already down to one-fifth of a second. Within a year after Daguerre's discovery a Viennese scientist developed a lens that remained virtually unimproved for half a century.

Itinerant artists, or "professors" as they came to be called, were at work in Canada by 1840. (At least one travelled with a phrenologist.) The quick growth of the profession has been carefully traced by Ralph Greenhill in his *Early Photography in Canada* (Oxford University Press, 1965), from which several of the factual details in this account are taken. By 1847 there was an established studio in Montreal and by 1849 another in Toronto. Niagara Falls, the most photographed of all Canadian natural phenomena, was then, as now, a mecca for professionals. A daguerreotype with a Falls background cost the subject five dollars, though by the middle 1850s the price had dropped to $4.50 which many a sucker, hooked by the pitchmen's promise of a fifty-cent print, decried as pure robbery. Elsewhere, as the craze died, you could be photographed for $2.50 in the popular two-and-three-quarter by three-and-one-quarter size. The very wealthy bought giant daguerreotypes, fifteen by seventeen inches, for fifty dollars.

The best of the professors did wonders for their subjects, plumping out sagging cheeks with cotton batting and pinning back protruding ears with sticking wax. Some even tinted their photographs, using coloured pigments and fine camel's hair brushes. Nobody ever did solve the problem of freckles, which stood out like black spots on the plate and could not be removed. By the late 1850s a new craze–the ambrotypes–caused the daguerreotype craze to decline, but a few daguerreotypes are still made today.

Ambrotypes, which had a brief vogue in 1855 and 1856, came about as a result of the collodian, or "wet-plate," process which Frederick Scott Archer, an English sculptor and photographer, presented as a free gift to the world in 1851. Ambrotypes were really underexposed negatives made by the new process, fixed and dried on glass and then set against a black background to appear as positives. Anyone can get the same effect today by underexposing a negative and looking at it by reflected light against a black background.

Ambrotypes were swiftly replaced by the cheaper tintypes, also made by the wet-plate process. Instead of glass, the plate was sheet iron and the need for a black background was eliminated by painting the metal black. These tintypes, often hand-coloured, could be made small enough to wear on a ring. They were mass produced in picture-mills that sprang up all over the country and were still being made, as late as 1900, in booths at country fairs.

But it was the paper photograph, printed from a wet glass-plate negative, that changed photog-

A late tintype, probably taken in the '90s.

An early amateur snap made at Sherbrooke, c. 1870.

raphy. Pictures could now be duplicated in quantity, reduced in size or blown up to enormous proportions. The very, very wealthy were prepared to pay as much as seven hundred and fifty dollars for a lifesize, hand-coloured portrait. The camera that produced these "Imperials," as they were called, was itself a monster. One of them had a thirteen-inch lens and a twelve-foot box, which may explain why so many of the subjects looked as if they were staring into the mouth of a cannon.

The paper photograph also allowed the mass production of stereoscopic views. We tend to think of the 3-D process as a modern development, but the first stereoscope was actually produced a year before the first daguerreotype. (Drawings, not photographs, were, of course, used in it). In the Confederation years the stereoscope was the craze of crazes. To anyone who picks up one of the old double prints and gazes at it through a century-old viewer, the magic will return. The very hairs on a man's nose reach out to you and the cliffs above Niagara's gorge seem real enough to topple from. Oliver Wendell Holmes, in his eloquent way, called the invention "a leaf torn from the book of God's recording angel," and all the world agreed with him. People spent evening after evening peering into stereoscopes and exclaiming over the vividness of the effects. Troths were plighted, friendships cemented and, no doubt, seductions effected simply as a result of two people squeezed onto a sofa gazing rapturously over and over again

at three-dimensional views of the Quebec Citadel or the Montmorency Falls. It is a craze that has never faded. All over the world to this day stereoscopic societies meet, print bulletins and issue portfolios of prints and transparencies, new and old, to succeeding generations of eager viewers.

By Confederation year, the photo business was ready to embrace planned obsolescence. So many people now had so many *cartes de visite* that the market was obviously saturated and the professional photographers were worried sick. A model-change was needed, and it came with the introduction of the new "cabinet size" photographs, which were no more than the old *cartes* enlarged to about double size. Everybody welcomed the new pictures, especially the album makers who instantly rushed a new model of their own into production.

Thus were the economics and techniques of photography suddenly changed. The warts and blemishes that had been so inconspicuous on the small photos stood out in the larger ones. In an instant the art of retouching was born. James Ryder, the Cleveland photographer who introduced it on this continent, later recalled that "it caught on like measles and became an epidemic." It was not enough to paint out a wen or an extra chin. Every middle-aged citizen wanted to look like his own son, and the retouchers cheerfully indulged the fancy. The critics, as usual, said that retouching would degenerate and demoralize the nation through its basic dishonesty; but the nation

Introduction

Early studio photographers posed subjects against painted backdrops.

survived and so did the retouchers—as any pimply adolescent who has posed for his high school annual knows to his relief.

The art of retouching in turn launched the art of gimmickry in portrait photography. From the Confederation era on, portrait galleries (the word "studio" was not yet in use) contained a bewildering variety of stage props: everything from toboggans to stuffed animals. Some years ago I had occasion to examine all the photographs made between 1858 and 1898 by the best known of the pioneer Canadian portrait photographers, William Notman of Montreal. There were thousands upon thousands of portraits, many of which seemed to have been taken out of doors in all kinds of weather, including blizzards. Yet I knew that every one of them had been made in Notman's studios.

As I leafed through the Notman prints I became aware of the presence of dogs in many pictures and it slowly dawned on me that it was always the *same* dog, a small, black spaniel with his head cocked to one side who, on closer inspection, was quite clearly stuffed. This stuffed dog, posed in a variety of ways with live subjects, was one of dozens of props that Notman used—hammocks, rustic bridges and gates, fake rocks and trees, painted backdrops and even ersatz snow. Notman was the number one snow-in-the-studio man of his day: he even sprayed some of his glass plates with Chinese white to produce the illusion of a storm. His liveliest Montreal competitor, James Inglis, was a water-in-the-studio man. He always kept a pool of real water under a skylight, ready to make a boating picture the minute a customer walked through the door.

Notman has left a description of his methods, describing the floor of his studio "which looks so brown and shabby to begin with that you never fear spoiling it, but, as occasion requires, with perfect freedom pile cordwood on it, build cottages, form sandy beaches with boats drawn up, erect tents, plant trees, crowd solid blocks of ice, form snow-wreathed plains or introduce a frozen lake or stream on which a skater may appear to glide. All this, if it does not afford a change of air, at least gives a change of scenery and by leading you out of the everyday rut invigorates and refreshes the mind."

If the photographers of those days entered into their work with zest, so did their subjects. People arrived with several costumes and were perfectly prepared to pose, not only in summer dress, winter dress and sports dress (with the appropriate lacrosse sticks or croquet mallets) but also in fancy dress. They acted parts, grimacing or glowering as the role demanded, portraying drunks, villains or beleaguered maidens. And this is all the more remarkable when one considers that each subject had to wait, occasionally for days, for the sun to filter through the gallery's skylight (no portraits were yet made with artificial light) and then hold a pose for anywhere from fifteen to forty seconds depending on the sun's intensity. Every gallery

One of William Notman's first composites. An 1872 children's production of The Merchant of Venice.

contained a variety of interesting if hellish devices –clamps, supports and metal posing stands that supported the subject's back, arms and head and thus rendered him reasonably immobile for the duration of the exposure. These were later removed by retouchers.

Under such conditions, the photographer himself had to be a master of ingenuity in order to retain some semblance of reckless spontaneity in his work. One man suggested the following recipe:

"Have at hand books, fans, flowers, ornaments, yellow-tinted letters filled with suggestions with which ladies can beguile themselves and their hands. Have canes, hats, pens and more books to ease off the angularity of the masculines. Provide jumping jacks, barking dogs, tin whistles, jew's harps, and a small organ to bamboozle the babies. Besides, be able *yourself* to turn into an acrobat, gymnast or long-tailed monkey on the shortest notice."

Under such conditions, group photography was virtually impossible. Yet the photographers of the day managed to counterfeit it. Through the device of the "composite" originated by an Englishman, Henry Peach Robinson, Canadians like Notman, Inglis and W. J. Topley of Ottawa achieved the impossible. Notman brought the composite photograph to its highest peak, often taking two years to prepare a single picture. Once he photographed twelve hundred separate figures and, with the aid of his staff of retouchers, many of them Academy artists, welded the whole into

Notman supported his figures on special stands for lengthy exposures and later painted out all props.

Introduction

a single magnificent panorama. Sometimes, indeed, it was difficult to tell where photography left off and painting began. Certain canvases of Montreal society's fancy-dress skating balls are actually composite photographs painted over.

The composite became obsolete in the 1880s with the invention of a new kind of photography, which permitted studio exposures of one-tenth of a second. This new photography arrived in a decade of scientific ferment. It is interesting to remark, in passing, that the development of Canada as a nation almost parallels the development of what can properly be called the modern world. This world began to emerge in the second decade of Confederation, between 1875 and 1880, when the slender Princess Shape was allowing a brief respite between the two bustles, and young bucks were driving around on high-wheeled velocipedes and singing *Listen to the Mocking Bird* to their sweethearts. These years saw the development in rapid succession of the telephone, the incandescent light bulb, the talking machine and the gasoline-powered internal combustion engine. They also saw the development of dry-plate photography, the method the world has used ever since to take pictures of itself.

The operative word is "dry." In this new process the photographic substance was made first and then applied as a coating to the glass plate. In the old wet-plate system it had actually been formed on the surface of the plate; by the time it was completely dry it was useless. But dry plates were ready for use any time. By 1880, George Eastman of Rochester was turning out dry plates for $3.60 a dozen. The same year a so-called "camera for the millions," a device complete with tripod and stereoscopic lens, went on sale for ten dollars. By 1884 Eastman had invented roll film. Four years later the word "Kodak" entered the language and a nation of shutter-bugs was born. "You push the button and we do the rest," the Kodak ads trumpeted, and hundreds of thousands did just that.

The dry plate made the work of the professionals immensely easier. Many of the frontier pictures which appear in the early sections of this book were made by men assigned to photograph the various surveys which were beginning to chart the dimensions of the new nation: the railway surveys, the boundary surveys and the geological surveys. Others were made by military men. One such gifted amateur was Captain James Peters, who commanded "A" Battery of the Royal Canadian Artillery during General Frederick Middleton's 1885 campaign against Louis Riel. Dry-plate photography made the picture on the opposite page possible. Peters carried one of the new "detective" cameras (a box camera *sans* tripod) on his back and, since he also had an artillery battery to command, often shot his photographs from the saddle.

"The fact that twenty percent of my men were killed and wounded in two engagements will be sufficient guarantee as to the indisputable fact of

Capt. James Peters used his "detective camera" to take this photograph of an impromptu barber shop at Qu'Appelle during the Riel campaign.

This composite, made by William Notman in 1885, shows an award winning Montreal bicycle club before the invention of the chain drive.

the plates being exposed actually in the fighting line," he reported, adding that none of the earlier cameras, with their awkward tripods, could have survived such a trip. Any man attempting to set one up, he said, would have been picked off instantly by the Métis sharpshooters.

Meanwhile, the studio photographers were growing wealthy. William Notman's Montreal mansion, complete with solarium and tennis court, rivalled those of the neighbouring railway barons in elegance. Out in Edmonton, the pioneer photographer Ernest Brown, who started taking pictures well before the turn of the century, was building up a minor fortune. By World War I his auditors valued his business at $265,000.

Brown was a genuine character who spent much of his time in a room crawling with live turtles, stuffed birds, hundreds of tinted pictures and enough Victorian bric-a-brac to stock a movie set. But he knew how to take and how to collect pictures and he caught the flavour of his times, as a glance at page sixty-seven will show. Brown had the foresight to buy up the plates accumulated by earlier competitors. As a result the Brown Collection today is the best in western Canada; without it, this would be a poorer book.

Like Brown, Harry Pollard, who set up shop in Calgary in 1899, bought plates from his predecessors. In 1965 his collection was purchased by the Alberta government for several thousand dollars. It is pleasant to report that Pollard was still alive to enjoy the windfall. It was not the

An early example of trick photography. The subject in each case is Edmonton's colourful Ernest Brown.

first time he had realized a profit based on fore-sight. When he came to Calgary he paid a few dollars for an earlier collection of glass plates, one of which turned out to be the original of what is undoubtedly the single most celebrated photo-graph ever taken in Canada–the driving of the last spike of the Canadian Pacific Railway at Craigellachie in the Selkirks. In 1907, the rail-way, which had only inferior copies of the famous picture, paid Pollard one thousand dollars for the original negative. Then it proceeded to hire him, for the next thirty years, to tour the world mak-ing field photographs for its travel posters.

At about the time that Harry Pollard was arriving in Calgary, photo-engraving techniques were being developed which would at last allow newspapers to print half-tone pictures. And in 1906 there arrived in Toronto from England, with just seven dollars in his pocket, five children in tow and a camera under his arm, the man who was to become the first great Canadian press photographer. His name was William James and he deserves to rank with the best. There are twenty-three of his pictures in this book and one has only to glance at them to know that James was a man ahead of his time.

James saw the Edwardian Age as if through the eyes of a man of the 1960s. He deliberately recorded scenes that make more sense today than they did then: shady lanes destined to become superhighways, obscure streetcorners on which notable buildings were later erected. It was as if

he had a crystal ball in his camera, and it is not surprising that so many Before and After shots of burgeoning Toronto make use of photographs by James.

James was careful to record the fashions of his day: the hobble skirt, the peekaboo shirtwaist, the Gainsborough hat. Though he himself refused to drive an automobile–he thought nothing of walking forty miles to Hamilton and back to make one picture–he chronicled with loving fidelity the rise of the flivver. In every sense he was a pioneer: he took the first candid photos in Canada; he made the first photographic abstracts; he took the first cheesecake pictures. He was forever photo-graphing the signs of his times–placards, price tags, theatrical posters, merchants' display cards. While others were making stiffly formal portraits of the well-to-do, or pleasant if somewhat arty shots of landscapes and buildings, or chasing am-bulances and fire engines, William James was photographing people, usually off-guard, at work and at play. From 1906, the year he won a twenty-five dollar prize in a newspaper photography con-test, until his death in 1948, this stubborn, proud and fiercely independent man never left his home without taking his camera with him. His photo-graphs, some of them more than half a century old, seem to have been made for a modern picture magazine.

There is no record that he ever photographed the one Canadian subject which, apart from Niagara Falls, has intrigued more people around the world than any other. The Dionne Quintuplets were the personal photographic property of James's younger newspaper colleague, the late Fred Davis. Davis's pictures of the quints were probably the most famous ever taken by a Canadian, with the sole exception of Yousuf Karsh's memorable wartime portrait of a cigarless Winston Churchill.

Davis took some of the first experimental colour photographs ever made in Canada. Although experimental colour work began as early as 1859, the first commercially practical film (a film, that is, which required a single exposure instead of several, as earlier films had needed) was not available until 1935, the year after the quintuplets were born. William James's son, Norman, chief photographer for the Toronto Daily *Star*, remembers the day when Davis brought back his first colour photographs of the Dionnes:

"He made a real production of it. When he had what he wanted he handed the prints around the darkroom. Everybody sucked in his stomach. They were brighter and sharper than any colour pictures I've seen since. For the 1930s they were fantastic. We put them down and started talking about the colour revolution. Then somebody picked them up again and the bubble broke. They had faded off to a kind of muddy grey; they weren't even good black and white pictures anymore. Davis spent I don't know how many hours trying to get the colour to stick, but he never did make it last long enough to completely dry."

Nonetheless, the colour revolution was on its way. Suddenly it seemed, in the years after World War II, as though every child of ten and every grandmother of eighty was snapping colour pictures—and pretty indiscriminately at that. As usual, in a new era of crazes which has run the gamut from the hula hoop to beatlemania, photography has continued to be the greatest craze of all.

I was reminded of this forcibly one June evening in the early 1950s after a flight of two thousand miles due north from Toronto to Pond Inlet on the very tip of Baffin Island. I had come with a party of scientists who planned to study the ecology of the Eskimo. Ours was only the sixth aircraft in history to land at Pond—on the ice of the Arctic Sea, a mile from the settlement. It was close to midnight when we arrived, the sun was still high in the heavens and, swarming towards us on dog sleds, came scores of Eskimos wearing seal-skin parkas and mukluks. I turned to one of my scientific companions and remarked that we had not only come two thousand miles north, but that we had also moved several thousand years back in time.

"You're absolutely right, of course," he said. "These are still a stone-age people, living in a stone-age culture and using stone-age implements. You are looking now at the primitive past. You'd better get out your camera."

I started to do so but I was too slow. One of the stone-age people, Brownie in hand, had already beaten me to the draw.

The photographer becomes an abstract artist

When Louis Daguerre made his first pains-taking scenic view, it was generally agreed that painting was dead—and so it was, in the form which the previous century had understood. The invention of the camera made non-objective art inevitable, for no painter could hope to rival the realism of the lens. Artists thus began to see things in nature which escaped the photographers; yet it was again inevitable that this new way of looking at objects and people could not long be confined to a single technique. Photographers themselves began to view the world in abstract. One who has done it remarkably well is a young Dutch immi-grant to Canada named John deVisser, who arrived in Toronto in 1952 and, after a spell in a department store camera shop, became a professional. In deVisser's eyes an exotic dancer, a harbour reflection, a wheatfield, a mud puddle, a hunk of Cana-dian Shield, a casement window, a river delta or a summer cottage all take on new shapes—sensuous, intriguing, mysterious —unappreciated qualities that also may apply to the nation as a whole.

Confederation Eve:
The nation seems to hold its breath

It is June 13, 1867, and the Ottawa Chess Club, above, is having its collective portrait made. It would be nice to suppose that the members, with their staring eyes and fixed expressions, are waiting with bated breath for the country to be born. Alas, the truth is less romantic: they are holding their breath, all right, but only because the photographer has told them to freeze for a full half-minute. One man, however, *is* holding his breath and has been since 1864, when the photograph below was made. He's Lord Monck, and he's always been an ardent exponent of Confederation. A grateful government is about to make him our first governor-general. Meanwhile, time exposure or no time exposure, Lord Monck and his retinue, being military men all, and thus used to a certain rigidity, seem serenely at ease.

1861: Hacking out the border

On the banks of the Moyie River,
in the heart of the Selkirk mountains,
a fresh furrow cut in the lodgepole
pines shows where Idaho ends and
British Columbia begins. (That's B.C. on
the right). Unshaven men with transits
and axes are already at work, as
they will be for another generation,
delineating the future shape of the
nation. They don't know that within a
fifty-mile radius of this point – later
to be traversed by a concrete highway –
a fortune in gold, zinc, lead and coal
lies waiting on the future sites of
Cranbrook, Nelson, Kimberley and Fernie.
In just three years, the prospectors
and the settlers will begin to stream
in. But now, six years before Confederation, this pinpoint on the map
is really at the very end of the earth.

1863: The age of wooden ships

On certain days a man can count as many as five hundred sail lying off Quebec City, waiting to load with sawn lumber cut from Quebec forests. As many as one hundred ships a year are built here. But the coming age of steam will shortly cost Quebec her place as Canada's second city.

31

1866: Fenian muskets rattle along the undefended border

Here are the Queen's Own Rifles of Toronto parading on the Champ de Mars in Montreal, in the days of crinoline, shawl and parasol. They are celebrating their successful rout of Fenian Brotherhood raiders who, in the interests of Irish independence, have decided to invade Canada as a base of operations against Britain. When the government called for ten thousand volunteers, fourteen thousand responded. The Queen's Own encountered eight hundred Fenians at Ridgeway near Fort Erie, and finally pushed them back into the U.S. There will be other raids, equally abortive, but they will have a certain value – giving to the scattered colonies and provinces a sense of urgency that will help push them into Confederation. The women's dress in this photograph is revealing: most fashionable women are now triangular rather than bell-shaped, and this profile is accentuated by a shawl draped over the famous hoop skirt and topped by the tiniest of hats. Already there is a slight emphasis on the ladies' behinds, which will lead, in another five years, to the first wild excesses of the bustle.

1867-1900:

THOSE HORSE AND BUGGY DAYS

The Canada that was born on July 1, 1867, was largely a backwoods nation of farms, villages and frontier settlements, as the pictures that follow demonstrate. It was to remain that way for all of the gaslit era we call "Victorian." The 1871 census shows that only twelve percent of the population lived in cities, of which only seven had a population exceeding twenty thousand. In the settled east, people for the most part inhabited a dark, rural world stitched together by a sketchy network of dirt and corduroy roads, and separated by stump fences and swamps that were alive with frog, mosquito and firefly. Women, whose place was definitely in the home, hand-milked cattle, hand-churned butter and hand-wove clothing. Mowers and reapers generally worked with scythe, cradle and oxen. If furniture and implements were locally made, so was recreation. Social life and honest toil were melded in a recurring round of barn raisings, corn huskings, quilting bees, threshings and sugaring-off parties.

The other great form of recreation was religion. From Confederation to the 1890s, Canadians were obsessed by the need for revival and redemption. In Ontario especially, Methodist churches, often incredibly ugly, speckled the countryside and the circuit rider was as familiar a figure as the itinerant peddler. Sundays were morguelike and even in the wicked cities the horsecars were stilled. Camp meetings ran for weeks as preachers warned against the pleasures of the flesh. Dancing was sinful, of course – especially the new waltz (*The Blue Danube* was the hit of 1867) which was more wicked than the quadrille or lancers. Smoking, card playing and makeup were sinful: only prostitutes wore rouge. Booze was perhaps more sinful than anything; and not without reason, for green whiskey sold by the dipperful for a few cents. If the Victorian Age in Canada was an era of croquet games, bustles, harness shops, toboggan parties, family picnics, band concerts, Prince Albert coats, moustache cups and minstrel shows it was also an era of drunkenness. In 1870, when Toronto's population was less than sixty thousand, there were two hundred tavern and saloon licences issued. Men literally toppled from barroom to gutter in full public view. In those days people actually did sign a physical pledge and wear blue ribbons proudly showing they were abstainers.

We look back on those horse and buggy days with some nostalgia; but life for all but a few was harsh by modern standards. The patent medicine ads promised sure cures for everything from lockjaw to cancer, but the doctors could not save George Brown's life when

an assassin put a bullet in his thigh. Smallpox, scarlet fever, diphtheria, whooping cough, tuberculosis and trachoma killed or deformed multitudes. The twin depressions of the age – in the 1870s and again in the 1890s – caused the rich to grow richer while the poor became poorer. There are two contrasting scenes from the 1880s which illuminate this class difference. One is of the workers on the Lachine canal striking for a raise in pay; they wanted a dollar for a ten-hour day instead of eighty cents – a demand surely designed to wreck the economy, as some said. The other is of the "swells," as they were called, parading up and down Toronto's King Street every afternoon between three and six, gossiping and exhibiting the latest fashions. They had nothing else to do. For such people the coachman was a status symbol along with the new tin bath tubs (hot running water was just coming in). A man of property could demonstrate his position in life by changing his clothes four times in a day: from single-button cutaway at eleven in the morning to four-button cutaway for dinner. And what a dinner! It could run to a dozen courses including pyramid of quail, suckling pig *a l'Italienne* and stuffed boar's head. We have inherited a slang expression from those times; it is "posh."

The class system was one of several heritages from the colonial era. That part of settled Canada which was not French was British to the heart. Private schools far outnumbered public schools in the cities. Military music, on the order of *Rule Britannia* and *Soldiers of the Queen*, vied with religious oratorios at band and philharmonic concerts. Patriotism and imperialism were part of every political speech. And yet a kind of creeping Canadianism was beginning to make itself felt. The first hockey game was played in 1875 and the Canadian National Exhibition became a reality two years later. Montreal, at least, was demanding a specific Canadian flag and the Marquis of Lorne, not without great difficulty, managed to launch a literary society with real live Canadian writers.

Out west a different kind of Canadian was in the making, produced by the rough democracy of the frontier and the new immigrant heritage. In the pre-railway days western life was incredibly primitive. Freight moved by mule or bull train, passengers by stagecoach. In the transient hotels, stranger bunked with stranger. The bathtub was unknown and even in the settlements the townspeople bathed nude in the chilly rivers. In their sod hovels, the homesteaders subsisted on a diet of bread, fat bacon, beans, dried apples, peaches, syrup, prairie butter and grease drippings. Getting drunk was the favoured recreation, outdoing such genteel pursuits as the spelling bee or the shooting match. Tobacco was universally chawn. Only with the coming of the women, many of them mail-order brides, did the amenities of civilization begin to appear. Prairie society began to blossom with engraved invitations, elaborate receptions and teas and other marks of culture. By the late 1880s even "lawless Edmonton" (so-called because it knew no civil law until 1890) had its theatre complete with dress circle.

We can glimpse something of those times, and sense how remote they are from our own, by leafing through the pages of the 1881 census and noting the occupations listed. For the west: freighter, muleskinner, bullwhacker, wheelwright, stageman, brickmaker; for the east: litterateur, trunkmaker, drayman, carriage builder, gilder, cooper, gunsmith, porter, saddlemaker and, of course, "gentleman of private means."

It seems, in retrospect, to have been a changeless period; and so it was by our faster-moving standards. Yet the Canada of the 1890s was far removed from the Canada of the Confederation years. By 1893, for instance, Montreal had introduced electric trolleys. In the larger centres, the party-line was becoming a social institution. The bicycle craze was at its height, bringing about a revolution in women's clothes. Roads were being gravelled and modern plumbing was making its appearance. Steam-driven farm machinery was changing the face of the west. The electric light, though still a novelty, had definitely arrived. The dime novel, yellow journalism, the comic strip, the Gibson girl, the Pullman car, the cakewalk, the celluloid collar – all these were minor footnotes to a changing age. Though the decade was anything but gay, it ended on a note of jubilance: gold in the Canadian Klondike beyond the wildest dreams of avarice; an eternal Queen celebrating sixty years of enthronement; and just over the hill of time the beckoning adventure of a new century.

The first bustle of the early '70s frankly accentuated those curves which the crinoline had concealed for two decades. The change in styles reflected social change. Women now had a kind of forward look.

Making a prime minister an honorary chief is an old
Canadian custom dating back to the birth of the nation.
Here, Sir John A. Macdonald, carnation in buttonhole and
looking properly modest, is honoured by the Six Nations
Indians in a ceremony at the Brantford Council House.

Confederation: The political years

It is April, 1868, and politics is already a fierce and
contentious topic in the brand new nation. One of the
Fathers of Confederation, D'Arcy McGee, struck down
by an assassin's bullet, is accorded an enormous public
funeral down Montreal's St. James Street. By nine a.m.
the streets are "crowded to suffocation" with sixty thousand mourners. The stores and offices are shut tight.
At least twenty thousand men march in the funeral pro-
cession, which takes close to three hours to pass by.

The 1870s:

In the Maritimes the great age of sail enters its final period

These pictures, all made in the early '70s, show New Brunswick and Nova Scotia at the height of their prosperity – wealthy societies thriving on the by-products of the age of sail. Maritimers not only build their own ships; they also own them, sail them and insure them. Saint John ranks fourth among the world's ports for registered wooden tonnage. In its twenty-five shipyards, thousands find work. But all this grandeur will start to fade during the next decade when steam begins to take over, followed by steel-plated vessels. Prosperity will end; a perennial dilemma will begin.

A forest of masts clog Saint John's harbour, but steam tugs are already in use. For those square riggers, the beginning of the end will come in 1885.

Saint John barque, *Edgar Cecil*, loads cannon at Halifax. The British are slowly withdrawing their garrison.

Above: On the Saint John River, genteel ladies can enjoy a croquet game without ever displaying an ankle. And few have heard of that terrible Mrs. Bloomer.

Below: A wedding in Halifax in the mid-'70s. The bridal gown with its outer corset is completely in fashion. Only the older generation now sports whiskers.

The covered wagons move west

Ox trains of the International Boundary Commission, mapping the border in Saskatchewan, snake through the prairie scrub at about ten miles a day. The commission has borrowed Napoleon's idea that "when the army can no longer nourish the oxen, the oxen can be made to nourish the army." It will be twenty years before the CPR at last renders the ox passé.

In far off British Columbia, camels and cattle invade a dying boom town

This is Barkerville, the great gold rush centre of British Columbia's Cariboo district in the early '70s, about a decade after the gold strike that made it the most flamboyant boom town in the nation. Originally a mining community, it is now giving way to the ranchers who have followed the prospectors into the province's interior. Already, the long-horned cattle have become a familiar sight in the mud of the town's famous single street. This one-mile clutter of clapboard, squeezed between hillside and creek, consists of saloons, dancehalls, hotels and stores, with a single opera house and an occasional church. Despite its gamblers, cowboys, miners and hurdy-gurdy girls, it is a law-abiding community, thanks to the so-called "Hanging Judge," Matthew Baillie Begbie. Its days, of course, are numbered. Barkerville will shortly become the nation's first ghost town, eventually to be restored as a monument to a raw and raucous era. But it has already served its purpose in opening up the rich hinterland of B.C. The stagecoaches, crammed with new settlers, are bumping along Sir James Douglas's fantastic wagon road, which links the coast with the Cariboo. The road builders included twenty-one camels, originally imported because of their packing abilities. Alas, their stench frightened off horses, mules and men alike and they were put out to pasture. The last of them is shown below, a bizarre footnote to the romantic tale of a region whose future will not be in camels or even in caribou – but in cattle.

In 1883, the last of the Red River carts makes its appearance on the streets of Winnipeg. Until this moment, most land freight has been hauled in these famous wagons. One of them pulled by an ox can transport as much as nine packhorses. For the past half-century and more they have been patrolling the plains in brigades, signalling their approach by clouds of acrid yellow dust and the nerve-wracking screech of wooden wheels rasping on ungreased axles. But the new railway, already in the building, has made the cart a museum piece.

The 1880s:
Steel makes the ox obsolete – and changes the nation

Now it's 1884 and there are twelve thousand men (and five thousand horses) blasting away at the Pre-Cambrian rock of Lake Superior's north shore. The CPR's William Van Horne has sensibly built three dynamite factories on the spot.

Here are the first Chinese in Canada – and even *they* don't know about chicken chow mein. They've been brought to B.C. to help build the railroad by a Mr. Andrew Onderdonk of California. *He* hasn't heard of the Yellow Peril.

Winnipeg, 1885: These soldiers are about to save the CPR from bankruptcy and the nation from Louis Riel. Mr. Van Horne is shipping them from Ontario to Saskatchewan. A grateful parliament will shortly vote another loan.

Those good old railroading days

Here is a photograph for railway buffs. This lovely locomotive with its huge stack, lamp and cowcatcher, built in 1873 for the old Intercolonial and purchased by the CPR in 1882, will do duty until 1895. By then it will, alas, be as obsolete as this timber trestle over the Nipigon River. But at this point (1886) steel bridges belong to the future. In order to push construction, the railway has spanned every gorge and canyon with timber cut on the spot.

Craigellachie, B.C., November 7, 1885: The last spike has just been driven and the famous official photograph has just been taken. Now the ordinary workmen who actually sweated on construction drive their own last spike – and pose for it.

If these Blackfeet are quizzical it's because the railway has ended a way of life.

This warlike Sarcee isn't quite as authentic as he looks. The portraitist has obviously loaded him down with every native prop at hand, to recreate the costume worn by the Plains Indians of the 80's.

Eastern volunteers snooze in trenches at Batoche, Saskatchewan, during the Riel Rebellion of 1885.

Human bones are relics of a Crow
Indian band, killed and quite
obviously scalped by the Piegans.

Blood and bones on the lone prairie

These mountains of bleaching
buffalo bones hoarded at railway
sidings by the ever perceptive Mr.
Van Horne are to be shipped east
to fertilizer factories to bring a few
more dollars for the hard-pressed
CPR. (Van Horne has got them
cheaply at seven dollars a ton.)
Such grisly relics are the result of
the white man's disastrous policy
of hunting down the buffalo *en
masse* for their hides only, using
repeater rifles rather than the
less efficient muzzle loaders
employed by Métis and Indians.

Ice is so thick on the St. Lawrence that passenger trains can cross it. The first excursion in January of 1880 carries 250 people to the Longueuil shore.

Ice is thicker, snow heavier and winters really are colder

Everybody's talking about the cold spell of the '80s. And it really *is* colder here in our great-grandfathers' era. In both Montreal and Toronto the average temperature is a full four degrees lower than it will be when Canada celebrates its hundredth birthday. It's true that temperatures have been generally rising since 1840 but they fluctuate from decade to decade. The '80s is one of the coldest periods of all. When people describe those terrible old-fashioned winters later on, they'll be right.

Sparks Street, Ottawa, in April, 1883, after one of the severest winters on record. The snowfall is almost two feet above average.

Mount Royal Park, 1889: If you can't lick the winter, join it.

The 1890s:

Booze is cheap and plentiful, the workday is long and everybody blows off steam

Down a long-forgotten street comes a pair of snorting firehorses pulling the chemical pumper that is to become a symbol of the era. These animals have been especially trained to run automatically into their traces at the sound of a clanging firebell.

Liquor of all kinds is cheap and easy to get, as this bottle-shaped kiosk in Montreal manages to suggest. You can buy a quart of cognac for one dollar.

The face of the 1890s is superficially gay, as these photographs show. Nobody thinks to make pictures of men and women starving in the streets. It just isn't news.

These people in Langenburg, Saskatchewan, have just finished helping Mr. Riedle, the immigration agent (extreme left) finish his home. A house-raising bee is always a good excuse for a bash, especially when beer sells for about six dollars a barrel. There's Mrs. Riedle (in bonnet) at the spigot and that's the town's first settler, Dave Berger (centre background), hoisting his glass.

New techniques and old traditions in the final decade of a dying century

The pictures on this page are an odd mixture of the distasteful and the nostalgic. We yearn for the days of the medicine man and mandolin. But when we recall the factory conditions and remember that the appendicitis operation was quite unknown, we all yearn a little bit less.

Here comes the medicine man, plying his potions in Saskatchewan, unrestricted by any food and drug regulations. He can and probably does advertise sure cures for everything from cancer to chilblains — with a free show thrown in.

The boiling room of Whitworth's candy factory in Edmonton has a distinctly Dickensian look. Factory girls are several steps below nurses, socially.

We're celebrating Queen Victoria's Diamond Jubilee of 1897 in Saint John, N.B. Some of us are entertaining ourselves in a new-fangled way with Mr. Edison's amazing talking machine—but others, more conservative, prefer to stick to simpler, time-tested methods.

We're watching a simulated operation in Banff in 1896. Sterilization is still a new technique. Anesthesia is primitive. There are no rubber gloves but nurses' sleeves are right in style.

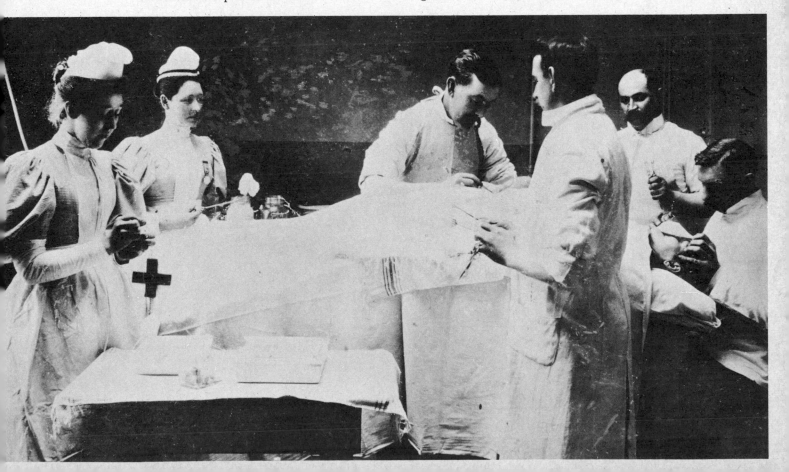

A placid era of horsecars and band concerts

We're on Yonge Street in Toronto at the corner of King, looking north. The horsecars are still running, but their days are numbered. By 1892, they'll be gone. Those arc lights, which were introduced back in 1884, will last until 1911. Isn't the traffic light? Just a few barrows and horse-drawn carts. No autos – yet!

On fine summer evenings, the Dufferin Terrace boardwalk in Quebec City is a mecca for strollers. Two or three times a week there's band music under those striped canopies and thousands turn out in all their finery to hear it. If you look down at the river you'll see one of the last of the three-masted barques.

In the back country, work and play take new forms

ABOVE These new agricultural contraptions, including the stationary thresher (left) and the steam traction engine (right), may look pretty ungainly, but with each small improvement they are changing farming methods. Mass production is twenty years away.

BELOW Though skirts still cling to the ground, women's dress is becoming a little simpler now that we're in the mid-'90s. And with good reason. Golf has just swept the nation, even here in the Quebec village of Petit Métis. The big change is coming.

Gold! It's 1898 and these men are among the hundred thousand poor lunatics trying to reach the Klondike by any means available; home-made sailing sleds, lines of mountain goats hitched up like teams of horses, yes, even bicycles. And each man must tote one ton of supplies with him or the Mounties won't let him cross the border – which explains the pile in the photograph above.

The Klondike Look

In Dawson City, women
like this one are as rare
as onions (which sell
in the drugstores
as medicine). Those who've
made it are as sturdy
and as serviceable as a
sled. After all they, too,
have had to scale
the passes. Many are
"actresses," a euphemism
that covers a variety of
duties both public and
clandestine. In the end,
this lady will dig more gold
out of men's pokes than
most miners will get from
the benches and bedrock
of Bonanza and Eldorado.

1900-1920:
THE AGE OF FAITH

It was truly the end of an era. The nineteenth century, the Victorian Age and the Boer War all wound up within a year of one another. The terrible depression of the 1890s was over, too. As the first decade of the new century began to unwind, the air crackled with fresh confidence.

A new phrase, "get rich quick," was entering the language though certain other words – bolshevism, boy scout, chauffeur, sundae, Rotary Club, no-man's-land, income tax and aspirin – had yet to be devised. Half way through that first ten year span, Col. John Bayne MacLean's new *Busy Man's Magazine* (a digest of articles soon to be re-named for its founder) began to expound the true religion of untrammelled enterprise: *. . . money is the handmaid of virtue . . . laziness is a disease – a pathological condition . . . if we do not struggle we will become weakened . . .* It was, obviously, an age of buoyant faith in hard work and rugged individualism when any youth could become prime minister, or, better still, president of one of those enormous corporations that were turning out a variety of newfangled gadgets: the electric chafing dish, the Excello power washer, the Diozo phone disinfector, the Parlograph dictating machine. The astonishments of the new age were mirrored in a popular saying: "There ain't no such animal!" But there *was*, of course. In an age that saw the invention of the airplane, the Victrola and puffed wheat, nothing seemed impossible. Even the most titanic ocean-going vessels were unsinkable. Or so it was claimed, in that dear, dead prewar age of faith.

The success of the Canadian Pacific Railway and the glitter of the Klondike had pulled men's faces around to the west and the north. New lines of steel were reaching across the continent and many more were planned. Out west, land prices were soaring more swiftly than Captain John McCurdy's *Silver Dart*.

Change, which was to become the great characteristic of the new century, began its acceleration in those early years. When the first decade dawned, kitchens and parlours were still lit mainly by candles and coal-oil lamps. Out west, families still crouched in huts of sod or poplar. The baroque, cast-iron stoves, constantly a-bubble with soups and porridges, were fired by wood. Save in the larger cities the roads were rutted nightmares. It was still the age of the livery stable, blacksmith shop and hitching post. Men shaved their beards with straight razors and women's skirts, plumped out with petticoats, trailed in the mud, dust and slime of the streets. Prices were low enough by today's standards: you could buy a turkey dinner for twenty cents and a muslin nightie for nineteen; you could rent a furnished room by the day for half a dollar. But wages were low, too: the swiftly multiplying breed of lady stenographers earned only ten dollars a week. Pleasures were simple: canoeing on a sleepy lagoon, bobsledding down a snowy slope, or bicycling along a shady lane with your baby-mine. The discomforts of those times have been long forgotten and only the serenity remains, captured in the durable song composed in the good old summertime of 1902, when words like "tootsie wootsie" were all the rage.

But there was a new restlessness in the wind and the new inventions, piling one upon the other, helped to spark it. The safety razor, the escalator, the nickel-odeon cinema and the flashlight (not to mention the banana split) had all come to stay. On May 13, 1914, wireless was born. And men were even starting to wear wristwatches!

The "new woman" of the 1890s was blossoming. The Anna Held fitted petticoat of 1905, with its scandalous emphasis on the hip, was followed by the equally scandalous peek-a-boo shirtwaist of 1908. In 1910 skirts at last began to rise, moving from ankle bone to boot top. By no coincidence, this was the first year of the electric self-starter. Women, freed of the handcrank, could at last drive cars – but their dress had to be simpler. What the bicycle had begun, the automobile and the new emphasis on women's sports was to complete. Basketball finally made the bloomer a commonplace. (The men were far more perturbed by the suffragette movement.)

In the relatively womanless west, the boom was on. In Edmonton the boosters were predicting a population of half a million by 1920. In 1911 lots on Jasper Avenue were selling for as much as two thousand dollars a front foot. When the Hudson's Bay Company divided up its six-thousand-acre reserve in May, 1912, some three thousand persons lined up to draw lottery tickets that would allow them to buy land. One man turned down fifteen hundred dollars for his place in line. Similar scenes were enacted all across the burgeoning prairies. The boom was the result of what Ralph Allen has called "one of the largest, noisiest and most successful medicine shows of all time" – the Canadian government's European campaign to attract settlers. From the Red River to the Rockies the population exploded from sixty thousand to one million in a single generation.

Then, in late 1912, the bubble burst. The bottom dropped out of inflated land prices. In Edmonton, seventy-five thousand lots reverted to the city in lieu of taxes, leaving a blank patch in the centre of town that was not filled until the 1950s.

What did Canadians talk about in those days? Often enough, the same things they talk about today: the flag, Senate reform, U.S. encroachment and, of course, wheat and the tariff. England was the mother country in every sense. Our major imports were from Great Britain and included school textbooks, foreign policy and Anglican bishops. There was a general feeling that Americans were vulgar as well as sinister and this was underlined in 1902 when the satirical Toronto monthly *The Moon* published a series of unflattering but wildly popular cartoons titled The American Girl.

Yet American culture was leaking across the border and there could never be enough fingers to plug the dike. The Victorian Age, which died hard in Canada, faded before Tin Pan Alley's new ragtime dances: the one-step, the fox trot, the turkey trot, the bunny hug and the puppy snuggle. In these syncopated caperings, designed to emulate the struts of animals, facing partners actually hugged each other. As a typical song of the Great War era maintained, "Everybody's Doing It!" – and some took it to mean more than just the Grizzly Bear. For another American import, the wartime assembly line, was having as great an effect on women's status, and hence the moral climate, as the dream of universal suffrage.

In the gumbo of Flanders, the men of the Canadian Corps dusted themselves with Keating's louse powder, clawed open tins of bully beef and the inevitable plum and apple, laughed at Bruce Bairnsfather's Old Bill ("When the hell is it going to be strawberry?"), cheered the Dumbells, grumbled at the Ross rifle and died. Those who came back were changed men. They had seen Paree and it was going to be hard to keep them down on the farm. (And less necessary, thanks to Massey-Harris.) They had seen Reality, too, and their faith was shattered. The age that had produced it – effervescent, trusting, oddly naive – was as dead as the polka; things could never be the same again.

In 1911 fashion enjoyed one last mad fling before the simpler styles came in. Brocade ran wild from hat to handbag, while thousands of ostriches were denuded to add a crowning touch to a gaudy wardrobe.

A distant war ends;
a new century gets underway

Here we are once again on Yonge Street in Toronto, looking north from King. It is now June 5, 1902, and the city is spontaneously celebrating the victorious end of the Boer War. The great bicycle craze, which has run unabated for a dozen years, is in its final stages. One Canadian out of twelve owns a bicycle, and many are buying the new models which have coaster brakes as standard equipment. The craze, which has caused saloons and theatres to close and cigar sales to drop, has brought with it a downtown parking problem plus changes in women's clothing. The ladies in this picture are all wearing shirtwaists, foulard ties and boaters in the best Charles Dana Gibson style. Boys as well as men are imprisoned in starched collars. The popular derby hat, or Christy Stiff, will be in vogue until 1915. The streetcars are horseless but the carriages aren't. If you look carefully you'll see two – complete with coachmen in toppers.

Gracious living in Edmonton, circa 1902

Things are beginning to look up on the frontier, where style is everything. But a glance at that china department shows that running water and electricity still belong to the future.

The well-stocked Edmonton Hotel boasts it's the finest west of Winnipeg.

Revillon Frères' china department: note oil lamps, bathroom basins.

Miss Montgomery's millinery store: the proprietor is seated at centre.

The La Prell home: the finest in a city of fewer than four thousand.

New developments in the century's first decade begin with the escalator, introduced by Eaton's. Sign indicates that sarsaparilla is still an "in" flavour.

It's 1905 and this is the nearest thing to a traffic jam that Yarmouth, N.S., can yet offer. That's a White steam engine puffing and blowing at the far left.

Nova Scotia, 1902: Alexander Graham Bell is madly experimenting with kites, hoping to invent the airplane. He will, too. But the Wrights will fly first.

Movies aren't respectable yet, but they're commendably short and cheap. Here at Toronto's Majestic, the show runs an hour, costs you no more than a cigar.

The harvest special, rolling west, briefly dumps its human cargo at Winnipeg. These men get better than two dollars a day – highest casual pay in Canada. Each one brings a suitcase full of sandwiches.

A party of Scottish immigrants arrives in Canada – heading out west.

The empty plains begin to fill up with strangers

The year is 1905 as the camera records an annual migration unique in the world. These casual labourers, photographed at Winnipeg's CPR station, are part of a vast army recruited back east to help harvest the early-maturing Red Fife wheat, which is changing the face of the prairies. Already, in five years, the crop has trebled. And because ten men must harvest what one sowed, the west is hungry for bodies. They pour in, transients and immigrants alike, crammed back-to-back in colonist cars. Thousands will make a stake and head east again. But the men in sheepskin coats will stick and build the west.

At Yorkton, in 1907, Mounties have to maintain order among crowds seeking to buy homestead land vacated by dissatisfied Doukhobors.

*The days that are no more:
Untouched, as yet, by war*

These photographs, all taken between 1900 and 1910, evoke memories of a simpler era before mass spectator sports, radio, the movies, the automobile and air transportation. This is the placid, unquestioning world of do-it-yourself fun that the Great War would change for all time.

Anybody can snowshoe and everybody does. It's *the* big winter activity. Who's heard of skiing? That sleeker sport fits a future age when snowshoeing will seem square.

On Montreal's famous mountain park, the tobogganers are as thick as snowbirds. These specially built, beautifully iced runs will soon be passé – along with the toboggan and bobsled.

8740—TOBOGGANING, PARK SLIDE, MONTREAL

It's 1909 and here on Toronto's Centre Island the egg and spoon race is a perfectly acceptable sport for senior teenagers. Except, in 1909, there's no such thing as a "teenager."

Here at Sunnyside beach, Toronto, the women are still wearing dresses, black stockings, shoes and hats to go swimming. They look just a little bit clumsy, don't they?

John McCurdy, Canada's pioneer flyer, wearing his hat on backwards in the accepted style of the day, poses amid a tangle of struts and wires. He's just made history at Baddeck, N.S., with the first heavier-than-air flight in Canada. In 1909, any red-blooded kid who can fly a plane can become the lieutenant-governor of his province. But who, except McCurdy, can fly a plane?

The air age begins as the decade ends

The women are wearing Gainsborough hats; the men are still in derbies and boaters, but they are all looking at the shape of the future. It's an unbearably hot day in July, 1910, and this is Toronto's first sight of a flying machine. The big air meet, which will last for several days, has just moved in from Montreal – the first of the great aerial circus displays that will dominate the coming decades. But the air age is not so advanced that a man can hop from city to city: the seven new-fangled machines on display here haven't arrived under their own power at all. They've come by train, dismantled and packed in crates. On this first day of the meet, Saturday, July 9, only three are in any condition to fly; but the results, shown above, are enough to cause intense excitement. There's a reporter in the crowd, scribbling away, and this is what he'll write: "They were not looking at anything resembling a bird at all but a great, wide monster, different from anything seen before on land or sea. In the air as it passed with a rush over the spectators' heads (for it cut across one end of the stand) it was hard to define what it looked like. One ingenious comparison was perhaps the best: 'Do you know,' said one man, 'it looks like the bridge of an ocean liner.' "

1910-1920: A wartime decade sows the seeds of future turbulence

The Great War generation is also caught up with boom and bust, traffic and women's status – an uneasy preview of the ferment that is to come.

May 13, 1912 – and Edmonton is going crazy over land. Three thousand line up all night for a chance to buy Hudson's Bay property. In a few months the bubble is going to burst.

These demure Toronto co-eds are as revolutionary in their own way as their suffragette sisters. They keep insisting on an education.

Yonge Street again, towards the end of the second decade. Here, at Queen, the traffic is starting to build up. Bicycles are on the wane; electric signs are coming in; but parking has yet to become a real problem.

We're in the city room of the Edmonton *Daily Capital* in 1912. Wanna bet those typewriters aren't still in use...somewhere?

Modern pictorial journalism makes its entry

These newspapermen belong to what is generally known as "the old school." That is to say they work long hours for very little pay in conditions of congestion and squalor. Spectacular advances in the art of photo-engraving have produced the modern illustrated newspaper and you can see some typical examples of early rotogravure pages tacked to the flowered wallpaper above. But newspapers haven't advanced to the point where they can provide so much as a shade for the solitary, naked bulbs that dangle over the typewriters. As for those early news photos – well, some of them will become valuable social documents, like the murder scene opposite in an old-time grocery store.

Parrsboro, N.S., July 5, 1919: this wartime Handley-Page bomber, having failed in an attempt to win a newspaper prize by flying the Atlantic, cracks up after a change of plan and promptly hits the front page.

These people have other things to worry about, but they're on the scene of Canada's biggest news story: the Halifax explosion, December 6, 1917. Dead: 1630; damage: $35 millions. And now a blizzard is raging.

The most fascinating thing about this 1918 photo of a murder in Edmonton isn't really the corpse but those old magazines (*Breezy Stories*, *Jack Canuck*, *Ainslee's*), signs, ads and labels — plus all those vintage corn-flake boxes.

1914-1918: Marching as to war

It's a kind of military axiom that a man without a uniform when set out on a parade ground and instructed in close order drill manages to look sheepish, scruffy and generally down at the heels. These are actually university professors, not condemned prisoners. But most will become leaders of men.

Aloft in his Curtiss-Jenny trainer, a would-be ace learns to use a camera gun in training. He engages in mock combat with his instructor and the camera records his degree of accuracy.

The scruffiness changes to spit-and-polish – at least behind the lines in Flanders where, by 1917, divisional concert parties (this is the Maple Leaf group) become famous. All of them feature female impersonaters, wearing the styles of the times. Other luxuries include actual baths, films – and *real* girls.

This kind of question on a billboard is enough to shame most civilians into joining the ranks. If you hold out, there will be a nice lady along at any moment to hand you a white feather.

Daddy, what did YOU do in the Great War?

JOIN NOW
Armouries-1 Block North

The world war ends; the labour war begins

It is June 21, 1919: Bloody Saturday in Winnipeg, which has suffered a general strike for the past five weeks. The paralyzed city is an armed camp and the violence that all have feared has finally

come. Before the day is out two men will be dead and thirty injured. These violent men, demonstrating before their city hall – beset by war nerves, labour grievances and vague hopes for a better post-war world – may not know it but they are creating history. Canada's only general strike will eventually be credited with giving birth to two new political movements: the Social Credit and the CCF Parties.

1920-1945:
THE FAT YEARS AND THE LEAN YEARS

No two decades in history are as clearly defined as those which lie neatly sandwiched between the world wars. Each has its own symbols and clichés. For the 1920s: bathtub gin, jazz, flappers and *twenty-three skidoo;* for the 1930s: breadlines, sit-down strikes, miniature golf and Benny Goodman. These were years of pendulum-swinging change in Canada; a predominantly rural nation in World War I, it had become an urban one by World War II. A British dependency in 1920, it was, by 1939, well on the way to becoming Americanized. For the entire Western world, these twenty years saw the acceleration of what has been called The Big Change—the revolution in morals, manners, attitudes and way of life that sets this century apart from all others.

In human terms the change is more discernible in women than in men. Consider, for instance, the matter of women's undergarments which, in 1920, were truly unmentionable. They then embraced such long-forgotten items as the envelope chemise, camisole, bodice, princess slip, corset, corset cover, combinations, bloomers, petticoat and drawers. Most of these vanished between 1920 and 1925—a period that saw dress yardage reduced by half. There are established cases of Victorian males fainting at the sight of an exposed ankle; but by 1925 the skirt had risen to the knee while the one-piece, skintight bathing suit was standard. It had made its appearance at Atlantic City in 1921 where, we are told, spectators "gasped" with shock. The gasps did not last long.

At the time the war ended, only actresses wore makeup. High heels and silk stockings were unknown. The suntan craze was still in the future. "The importance of keeping skin and hair from being sunburned cannot be too much stressed," *Vogue* told its readers in 1919. It was as unthinkable for a woman to cut her hair as it was to smoke a cigarette. All this was swept away in half a decade. By 1924, even the Methodists had raised their ban on dancing. Night clubs were invented, along with cocktails. *Vamp, sheik* and *gigolo* had entered the language. Jazz, which one Canadian magazine writer called "a moral smallpox," was permanently entrenched. And sweet, innocent little Mary from University Avenue, Toronto, had been replaced by Clara Bow, the It girl, as America's sweetheart.

For anyone past middle age those years come back dimly in a succession of fuzzy flashbacks: the day your mother got her hair bobbed . . . the smiling Prince handshaking his way across the west ("Someday you will reign over the greatest Empire in the world," Premier Taschereau told him in Quebec) . . . listening to the radio through earphones on the CNR train . . . getting a medal on Dominion Day, 1927 . . . the song called *That's My Weakness Now* . . . Whoopee suits and twenty-eight-inch pant cuffs . . . orange phosphate and wire soda-fountain chairs . . . being angry at Americans who said: "We won the war" . . . being baffled by grownups discussing the *I'm Alone* case.

The *I'm Alone* was a Canadian rum-runner sunk by U.S. Coast Guard cannons; the incident was an international *cause célèbre* for most of the prohibition years. Most of Canada was wet in those days, and some substantial fortunes were made shipping illegal booze across the Detroit River or the Saskatchewan border. In the first year of the Great Thirst, Canadian whiskey imports quadrupled, but Canadians drank only a fraction of it.

The hangover that followed was worse for Canada than for any other nation. For the people of the prairies, where drought struck six years running, it was worst of all. The depression did something to Canadians and even today those who lived through it bear its psychological scars: they hesitate to buy on time, they dislike mortgages, they are a little over-obsessed with the need for a nest egg. Yet one's memories of the 1930s, mellowed as always by time, are remarkably warm: Technocracy . . . jitterbugs . . . freewheeling . . . flagpole sitting . . . *Skippy* . . . fireside chats . . . the Big Apple . . . knee action . . . self-serve groceries . . . crooners . . . the Dionnes . . . contract bridge . . . nickel milkshakes . . . the abdication . . . *Doc Savage* . . . the Miller stork derby . . . the two-piece bathing suit . . . Little Audrey jokes . . . the death of Will Rogers . . . the Fleischmann Hour . . . Eugenie hats . . . Clark Gable without an undershirt . . . chain letters . . . *Pennies from Heaven* . . . Torchy Peden . . . Knock, Knock jokes . . . Bank Nite . . . Renate Muller in *Sunshine Susie* . . . Baby Austins and Airflow Chryslers . . . Confucius Say jokes . . . and optimistic signs saying "Wasn't The Depression Awful?" What a crazy, mixed-up, wonderful, distressing, painful and unforgettable era it was!

It was a time when everything was streamlined, when all the angular artifacts of the 1920s—from coffee tables to girls—took on curves again. Even the modern houses had curves, including curved corner windows. The actual phrase was "modernistic" and that adjective is as dated as the architecture it describes.

The work week, for those who worked, was growing shorter, thanks in part to the new technique of the sit-down strike, and so sport, once the preserve of the moneyed classes, reached out to the masses. Skiing began to soar in popularity but the most popular sport of all was softball, which women could play. The spectator sports were on the rise. Ted Reeve might complain that the Americans were taking the foot out of football, but the American-style game was starting to pull ahead of its English counterpart. At about the same time, the German-made miniature camera was invading the land and the candid camera craze was off and running. The picture magazine, with its grainy but oddly realistic photos of unposed celebrities, became the publishing phenomenon of the age. A comparison of the photos on pages 53 and 107 shows just how much the miniature camera changed photography.

It was, as might be expected, a cynical enough era. The phrase that sums it up is the one that came into vogue in the early 1930s: "Oh, yeah?" Yet it was also a time of idealism, much of it misplaced. It was almost fashionable to be a Communist and certainly respectable to be a pacifist. University students by the thousands swore they would never fight for King or country.

But fight they did, and die by the thousands, too, at Dieppe, Falaise and Hong Kong, in the war that followed. For thousands more it was a war of waiting around, so that half the memories of those days have nothing to do with fighting. They involve meatless Tuesdays and arguments over the Zombies and getting your teetotalling grandmother to buy a liquor permit. They have to do with Glenn Miller's *Sunrise Serenade*, Betty Grable pin-ups, Lorne Greene's voice on the ten o'clock news and the dank smell of perspiration in the crowded bunkhouses of the basic training centres. They are compounded equally of small miseries and minor ecstasies: the first short arm inspection, the first TABT reaction, the first forty-eight hour pass, the first parcel from home. *Get cracking . . . put me in the picture . . . what's the gen? . . . pranged a kite . . . gone for a Burton . . . my shattered category* – the old phrases are as haunting and as far away now as a bugle call. Was it really so very long ago, this era of B-girl and Bren gun, Zombie and gremlin, black market nylons, war brides and Kilroys? Scarcely twenty years have passed since those days of victory, V-E and V-J, but so much has been crammed into them that already it seems a lifetime.

Of all the ephemeral styles of the past century, those of the 1920s are the most instantly recognizable: cloche hats, bobbed hair, knee skirts. Again one has to ask the women: How could you?

The 1920s: Canada becomes a smugglers' haven. It's the start of the Roaring Decade and Canadians are making money out of the Great American Thirst. Boatloads of hooch head off for "Peru" and return in two days. Some kind of new speed record? Hardly. Just forged receipts.

This man is a walking speakeasy. He strolls past the customs muffled in one of those '20s overcoats, and nobody wises up.

By 1925 Canada slowly awakens to the fact that this girl can also sneak stuff *back*.

Nova Scotian rum runner *I'm Alone* is about to cause an international incident. She's bound for the Gulf of Mexico where, on March 22, 1929, in the tenth year of prohibition, the U.S. Coast Guard will sink her – and then wish they hadn't.

On the Detroit River a runner with binoculars awaits a signal before he dispatches a speedboatload of whiskey to the U.S.

Detroit police smash crates of liquor with axes. This scene is the exception. Thousands of bottles are getting by.

The nation begins to jazz up

It's 1922 and the call of the saxophone is heard in the land. Here are the Elks Junior Musicians of Winnipeg. Those gymnastics aren't really necessary, but the players obviously think they somehow help the new sound.

Booze of any kind, save for "medicinal" purposes, is banned in some parts of Canada, though stills like this one, seized in Manitoba in 1922, operate more or less secretly. Dry from 1916, the province will go mildly wet in 1928.

By 1925, John Bracken, the premier of Manitoba, is able to make a pioneer broadcast right from his home. What passes for a network is controlled by the C.N. Railway. It's so formal some announcers come in black tie.

A softball game in downtown Toronto: women, eager to indulge in men's sports, have made this the most popular of all – and everybody from royalty on down wears plus-fours. Yes, that's a Model-T back there beyond first base.

The Americans have just invented the beauty contest and we're eager to grab hold of a good thing. Here, the first Miss Toronto contest, 1926. Some of the contestants still insist on keeping their knees covered – which maybe isn't such a bad idea at that.

Yes, those familiar hooded figures with the maple leaf badges are Canadians. It's July 1, 1927, and almost everybody else is celebrating our Golden Jubilee. But here in Kingston, our first capital, the Klan is gathering "to awaken the conscience of Canada"– whatever that means. Like the beauty contest, the Klan is an American import, but fortunately it won't last as long. Right now, however, it's spreading like wildfire with more than fifty thousand members across the land, and especially in Saskatchewan. Its chief targets, as you'd expect, are Roman Catholics and Jews. Incidentally, it insists on spelling Canada with a "K".

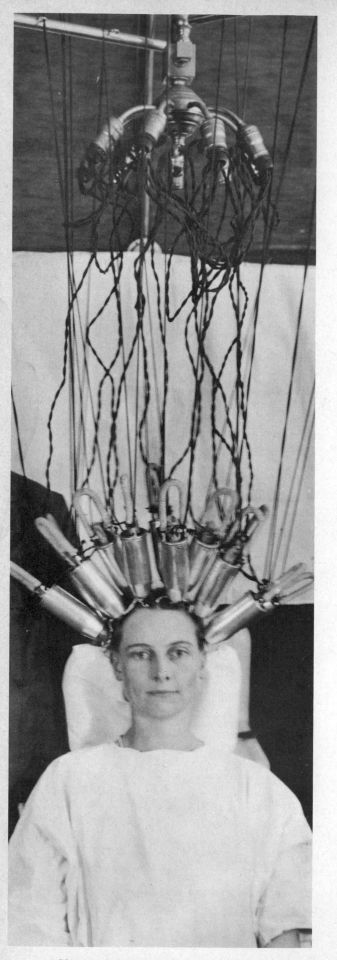

Shape of the new decade clearly emerges as Eaton's opens its beauty salon with a new apparatus for permanent waves. About 1920.

As any red-blooded Harold Teen fan knows, ice cream parlours are "in" in the '20s. But sarsaparilla seems to be out. Those milk shakes actually *are* shaken by hand.

1920-1930:

We're watching a boat driven entirely by radio. It's a novelty, used as a promotional gimmick by a newspaper, and it won't last long in this form. But some day the same idea will be used on everything from moon rockets to Japanese mechanical toys.

The whole country's gone airplane mad. This lady has just arrived at Thorncliffe track in Toronto. She's a Van Horne, and you can bet the old railroader is revolving in his tomb.

As the decade ends, the talkies come in. The name won't last. The talkies will, but this oldie won't make the late nite show.

The winds of change blow down the decade

As the new decade begins, miniature golf emerges as the craze of crazes. This course is in Winnipeg.

The 1930s: Years of drought and despair

This is a farm near Cadillac, Saskatchewan, in the mid-depression years; but it could be anywhere in southern Alberta, Saskatchewan or Manitoba. The lush wheatfields, parched by lack of rain, have become a Sahara, given over to grasshopper and Russian thistle, plagued by hailstone and rust. More than half the families are on relief; most municipal councils are bankrupt and even the reeves and council members are on the dole. The topsoil, blowing with the wind, has become a black blizzard in the sky so that even those who can afford to are afraid to sink a plough into the land for fear it will all drift away. All over Canada, demoralized men are drifting like the prairie soil; new political forces are being shaped; a future welfare state is in crucible. But this is small comfort to those who must eke out life here in the "Bennett barnyards."

These ravenous men lining up for grub in a Port Arthur soup
kitchen, have just been thrown off relief by the provincial government. The city, facing a sitdown strike or worse, has accepted
Mayor Cox's offer to use cooks from his lumber camps and
feed them. Six hundred get two more-or-less square meals daily.

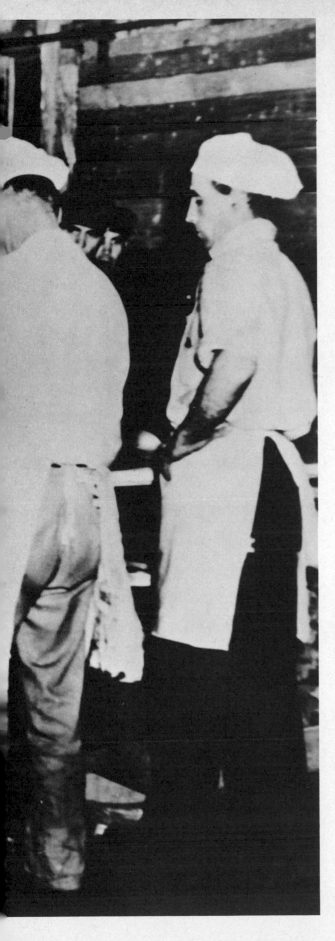

This is the symbol of the times — an engineless auto, permanently out of gas, a horseless carriage gone back to horsepower. It's derisively called a "Bennett buggy" after the plump corporation lawyer who suffers from the great misfortune of being prime minister during the worst economic crisis in our history.

Hunger, violence and derision stalk the land

It's Dominion Day, 1935, in Regina, but the flags have all been torn down by men who want action, not slogans. Two thousand relief workers are in open warfare with the Mounties. One hundred stores have been damaged. Ten persons have been wounded and forty more arrested. But the depression still goes on.

It's October 30, 1930, and the Eaton family is emerging as one of the world's richest. Here comes young John David, the new boss – orchid in buttonhole, golden key in hand – all set to open a new Toronto store on College Street. Lady Eaton is with him.

This picture needs no caption. The little girls, born on May 28, 1934, will soon be as well known as any princess or movie star – and their public goldfish bowl will be no less transparent.

July, 1935. Red Ryan, Canada's most notorious bank robber, thanks Father Wilfred Kingsley, the prison chaplain who secured his parole. Ten months from now, he'll be dead of a police bullet, having neatly betrayed all of those who tried to help him.

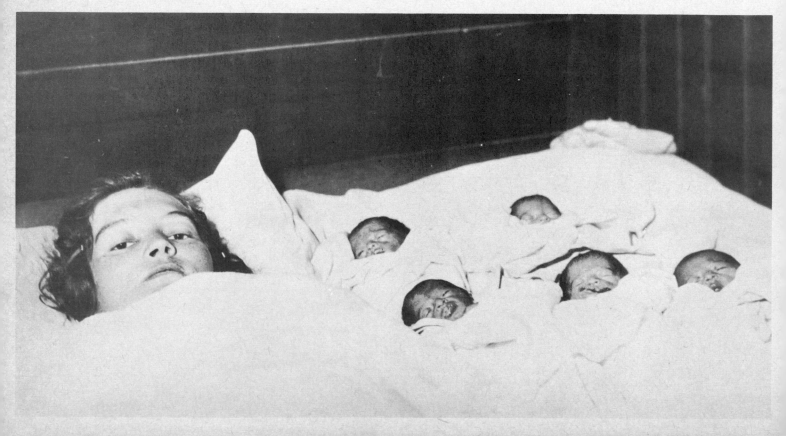

April, 1936. The CBC's Frank Willis, at the scene of the Moose River mine disaster, broadcasts without let-up to a world waiting for news of three trapped men. Two survived.

April, 1939. Footloose this time in Outer Mongolia, Gordon Sinclair continues to make as much news as all his colleagues combined.

It's 1937 and Bible Bill Aberhart, premier of Alberta and head of the world's first Social Credit government, is at the height of his power. The province is already cluttered with foreign newsmen trying to unscramble his heady political doctrines.

The King is dedicated, shy and sometimes just a bit cranky, but the Queen is a living doll. How neatly the decade winds up!–with a kind of fairy tale party before the new war begins.

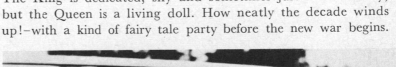

This is an amateur picture, incidentally, and it will make a small fortune for a young University of B.C. student named Ted Underhill. Published in the press, it somehow captures the public fancy as no other single photo does. He'll sell thousands.

1939-45:
Keeping the home fires burning again

These boys are Canadians not by choice but by the circumstance of war. They are "war orphans"– evacuees from beleaguered Britain. And fanatical Maple Leaf fans, too.

This tired Quebec foundry worker, one of Canada's enormous wartime labour force, is taking a nap – or so the National Film Board caption says. More likely he's been posed.

This "lumberjill," left, going to work in the Queen Charlotte forests of B.C., is forcing a social change. The per capita female labour force will double in this decade.

Here are Sergeants Johnny Wayne and Frank Shuster, two of the stars of the Canadian Army show, which did so much to boost civilian morale. In this war, you'll note, they're using real girls.

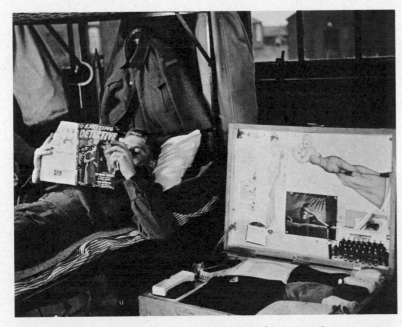

The pretty girl, the pin-up and the pulp magazine are part of every soldier's kit. This is a bunkhouse at Currie Barracks, Calgary. The author of this book slept not far away.

In Dawson Creek's single beer parlour, a group of American workers helping to build the Alaska Highway indulge in an old Canadian custom. Smiling is okay; but all other joy, including singing and eating, is against the rules.

Paper blizzards across the nation mark Germany's defeat

It's V-E Day in Canada and all across the land Canadians are indulging in those semi-spontaneous demonstrations which usually take some time to build up. (Fortunately, the press has been reporting the German surrender since the previous afternoon.) In Halifax, the news has touched off the worst riots of the war – three million dollars damage and some two hundred arrests. The rest of the nation is more jubilant and less bitter (though even here in Toronto the queue of people seeking housing accommodation remains unenthusiastic). In Montreal it's snowing real snow. Elsewhere the blizzards are paper. Well may Bay Street indulge itself: the postwar era is about to bring on the greatest stock market boom in the country's history. And yet the people, scarred by the horror of the 1930s, cautiously await a new depression.

1945-1965:
THE NUCLEAR AGE

Though history will probably name it the nuclear age, there are other equally accurate terms for it. It is certainly the space age and it is also the jet age. It is the TV age as well as the age of suburbia. It can be the instant age, the beat era, the sick epoch depending on one's point of view. Its temples are the supermarket and the shopping centre, its artifacts the directional aerial and the barbecue, its nostrum the tranquillizer, its high priests that venerable trio of doctors: Spock, Kinsey and Peale.

It is hard now to realize that until the new era arrived, the world was without wonder drugs, plastics, aerosol containers, LP records, DDT, ballpoint pens, birth control pills, drip dry suits, aqualungs, TV dinners, home permanents, Polaroid cameras, computers, Xerox copiers, stainless steel blades, picture windows, filter tips, automatic transmissions and transistors.

It is hard also to grasp the domestic revolution. The "young marrieds," as they came to be called, lived quite differently from their parents. The Canadian parlour was virtually extinct, replaced by patio and living-area. The sit-down dinner party vanished in the wake of buffet and cookout. Sideboard and closet yielded to built-ins; oak gave way to teak; and everything, from TV to toenails, from bathtub to kitchen sink, was in living colour.

The Canadian Sunday was as dead as the Canadian front porch, swept away on the wave of a revolution in morals that placed *Fanny Hill* within the reach of every moppet and made the bare bosom as familiar as a shirt front. Few people rested on the seventh day. They engaged in do-it-yourself work, thanks to the power tool craze, or do-it-yourself play, thanks to the speedboat-sports car-snowmobile craze. Wilderness lakes, once reserved for Group of Seven sketchers, reverberated to the echo of outboards, the sale of which increased six-fold between 1950 and 1965. That distinctive Canadian invention, the Peterborough canoe, was rendered obsolete by fibreglas. And that peculiar Canadian institution, the summer cottage, with its wide verandahs and its dusty stack of old Victrola records, was suddenly transformed into a triangular pre-fab complete with hi-fi. Fed by the thirty-five-hour week and the twenty-one-day vacation, summer cottageland reached out in ever-broadening ripples toward the distant tundra.

Canada had become a nation of cities and encircling suburbs – and more interesting cities at that, thanks to the new immigrant wave and the affluent teenagers. By 1961, seventy percent of all Canadians were urban dwellers. Only twelve percent lived on farms. It was a vastly more complicated life than the nation had known back in the days of the quilting bee. Traffic, alcoholism, juvenile delinquency and something called "the rat race" were its concomitants.

The pull of the cities made it the Age of the Big Shift. Never before had so many Canadians moved from pillar to post. When the head office beckoned, families thought nothing of pulling up stakes. Once in the big city they were likely to move twice more in a decade – first to one suburb, then to a more fashionable one. In Toronto, a city of home owners, the average man stayed in one place less than five years.

The commuting was spectacular. Businessmen thought nothing of popping into Ottawa or Toronto from Montreal and back again for dinner. One TV performer, Elaine Grand, spent most of a winter commuting between Toronto and London. Another, Joel Aldred, commuted weekly between Toronto and Hollywood. An actress, Kate Reid, commuted twice weekly between Toronto and Broadway. Thanks to the new leisure, the new affluence and the new chartered flights, Canadians of modest means began to see the world. And this, in turn, contributed to the end of the Mackenzie King isolationism that had characterized the prewar years.

What did Canadians discuss in the years following the war? Well, they talked about Barbara Ann, royal tours, the Boyd gang, the pipeline debate, the Dewline, the AVRO Arrow, the "quiet revolution," Gunnar Gold, the Bomarc, Mom Whyte, Joyce Davidson, biculturalism, the flag debate, Robert Goulet, Diefenbucks, conversational French and Lucien Rivard.

But more and more, in spite of a vigorous if wistful quest for a distinctive national identity, they seemed to talk about the same things Americans talked about. They talked about subliminal TV, the Edsel, Davy Crockett, Asian flu, widescreen, the Bold Look, McCarthyism, men of distinction ads, flying saucers, be-bop, Jayne Mansfield, motivational research, Zen Buddhism, Rita and Aly, sick comedians, Lizenmike, freedom fighters, Arthur Godfrey's humility, method acting, *Confidential*, vodka martinis, Jack Paar, painless childbirth, infectious mononucleosis, the Bolshoi Ballet, Volkswagens, Ivy League suits, LSD, the sack dress, *Playboy*, nymphets, cholesterol, radioactive milk, Lizeneddie, tinted hair, chlorophyll, grey flannel suits, the cha-cha, status, tail fins, royal jelly, eggheads, teenage werewolves, apartheid, *Mad*, smellovision, the thinking man's filter, the Dead Sea scrolls, the jet set, squares, beehive hair-dos, *Why Johnny Can't Read*, mods and rockers, adult colouring books, elephant jokes, non-violence, Lizendick, the new maths, discotheques, pop art, *The Feminine Mystique*, beatlemania, and high school dropouts.

And they discussed Health, fiercely. The diet craze ran on unabated. Thousands vainly tried to stop smoking. Men did 5BX. Though people were living longer and half a dozen major diseases (such as TB, polio and strep infections) were conquered, Canadians took more pills than ever before. Between 1950 and 1960 the sale of vitamins doubled.

Because we are part of it, this new age seems more terrifying, sobering, nervewracking and downright ill than those past eras which we like to believe, in retrospect, were Golden. At times the country has seemed about to blow up, fly apart or simply go down the drain. It is too soon yet to see our own times through the honey haze of nostalgia. Yet it is possible to sense that these, too, have been golden years and that, a generation from now, certain memories will return to haunt us: songs like *Moon River* and *Dear Heart* . . . Shirley Harmer on television . . . Scrabble games played *en famille* . . . barbecue parties around the new swimming pool . . . an Al Hirt album on the hi-fi . . . summer evenings at the drive-in . . . winter skiing in the Laurentians or on Grouse Mountain . . . . those wonderful Grey Cup parades . . . old, dated sayings like Cool it, man ! or Endsville ! . . . the memory of a vintage Mustang ("now *there* was a car !") . . . old-fashioned black and white TV . . . the world's fair in Montreal . . . Mr. Diefenbaker stumping the country . . . rocking 'round the clock ("did people really dance like that?") . . . coffee house bull sessions on existentialism . . . open line programs on radio ("whatever became of *them?*") . . . and those bright nights filled with promise when, staring up into the stars, we saw the silver-dollar shape of a new satellite drifting across the heavens and beckoning us into the next century.

The bikini bathing suit—closest thing yet to public nudism—was the most significant change in feminine fashions in the postwar era. It's significant that its very name—not to mention its impact—was nuclear.

Postwar: The Italians transform Hogtown

Old Torontonians may roll in their vaults but, yes, this *is* Sunday. This new private park is known as the Italian Pleasure Gardens. Very un-Torontonian.

Can this be Orange Toronto – actually celebrating Corpus Christi Day? Yes. But the city proper, once a Protestant bastion, is now half Catholic.

Can this be Canada? Obviously these two young persons, blatantly gambolling in the grasses in full camera view, weren't raised to Our Way of Life.

The language of love is demonstrably foreign, as are the signs. Nearly two hundred thousand Italians are now hived in Toronto, mainly in this one area.

New leisure spawns new fads

The tourists panning their own gold at the Dawson City Festival, and the eighty-five hundred Ottawa bingo players below, symbolize two postwar phenomena: the culture craze and the gambling controversy, both products of a new, affluent, leisure society.

A skating rink in the heart
of the financial district: a
city hall that is actually sexy:
what's happening to Canada?

What's happening is that
the country is growing more
broadminded as it grows
wealthier. Something else
is happening, too, reminiscent
of the previous century:
now that people have more
time on their hands, they're
starting to make their own fun.
Even the mayor of Toronto
can be seen here on a Sunday,
skating away.

New forms of sport grab the spectators

A snowmobile rally at Lake Chemong, Ontario, brings one hundred and sixty entrants from both sides of the border. The result of wartime research, the snowmobile is a uniquely Canadian form of transportation.

Grey Cup fever is at its most feverish here at the CNE stadium in 1962, when the west beats the east by one point. Score: Winnipeg, 29; Hamilton, 28.

Mosport, the new sports-car track in Ontario, can cram in as many as fifty-two thousand people on a big day. The new superhighways handle as many drivers, and most of *them* seem to think they're at Mosport.

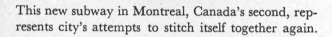

This new subway in Montreal, Canada's second, represents city's attempts to stitch itself together again.

City dwellers, recalling a rural childhood, respond nostalgically to sylvan siren songs like this one.

Suburbia reaches toward the frontier

A decade ago, this incongruous picture would be unthinkable: two status dogs going for a suburban stroll
at Wabush, deep in the remote heart of Labrador.

A retail revolution transforms shopping

The supermarket concept can be applied to almost anything: used-car lots, cut-rate emporiums or an entire business district – which is really what Toronto's Yorkdale is under a single roof. This great plaza with its eighty acres and one hundred odd stores is a long way removed from the Piggly Wiggly or Loblaws of our youth.

In the hands of "Honest Ed" Mirvish, the old-style cut-rate store becomes a vast and garish emporium selling everything from penicillin to golf clubs.

Every large city now has its own used-car "strip"– a gaudy, raucous roadway of hard-sell car marts.

Glossy new Yorkdale centre boasts "invisible door" —an air barrier that shuts off outside temperature.

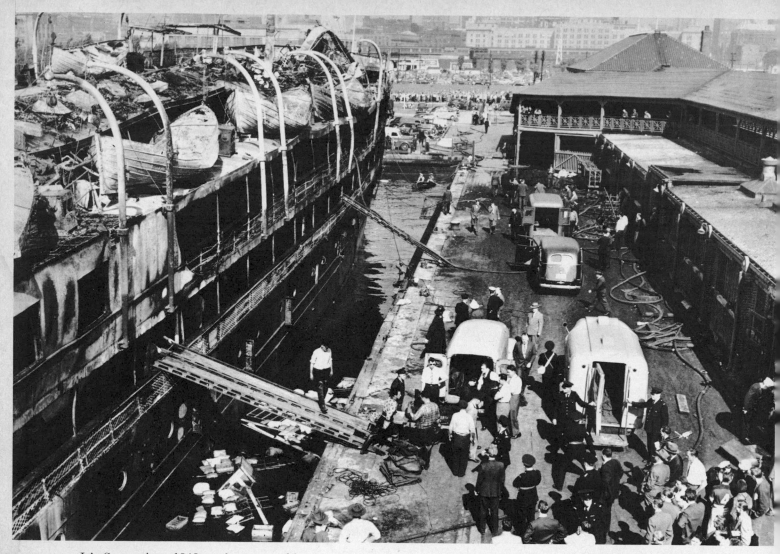

It's September, 1949, and a wave of horror envelops the nation with the realization that the *Noronic*, largest Canadian passenger vessel ever in service on the Great Lakes, has been gutted by fire. One hundred eighteen souls have perished. Soon after this, all passenger traffic on the lakes will end.

The disasters we'll always remember

It's May, 1950, and the postman on the right is making his rounds in Winnipeg, a good chunk of which is under water. Eighteen thousand homes are flooded, ninety thousand people have been evacuated and the damage is estimated at twenty millions. The flood, eighth since 1826, was predicted by one or two Cassandras but, as usual, few bothered to heed them.

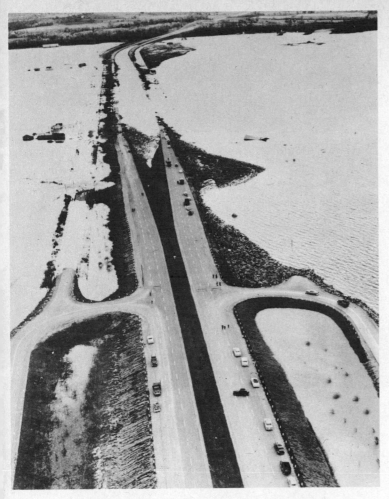

October, 1954. The rich Holland Marsh lies under water as Hurricane Hazel takes 82 lives in Toronto.

October, 1958. At Springhill, N.S., 174 coal miners are trapped. Rescue workers (below) manage to save 100.

February, 1959. Thirteen thousand are jobless as Canada scraps the Arrow. The plane above is junked.

May, 1963. One of the bombs placed by separatists in Montreal mailboxes mutilates Sgt.-Major Walter Leja.

In Toronto, university students demonstrating before the U.S. consulate over racial strife in Selma, Alabama, sit out a spring blizzard.

Separatists demonstrate as Montreal's new Place des Arts opens.

Saskatchewan citizens demonstrate before legislature during fight over health plan.

The 1960s have arrived and something is happening to Canadians. They are starting to get excited about such issues as medicare, nuclear weapons, separatism and race. The fat, complacent postwar era is over.

"Peaceniks," using non-violent techniques, demonstrate before RCAF Bomarc missile base north of Montreal.

TV provides the nation with a burgeoning new industry

There are 124 talented people in this picture. It takes all of them to put a single program onto your home screen – in this case the Wayne and Shuster hour. In radio, it took 20 or fewer. TV's enormous cost brings complaints. Yet it may well spawn a healthy Canadian film industry and bolster our theatre, too.

*In the coffee houses
a new generation
of Canadians begins
to emerge*

Here is a picture of Canada
that did not exist a decade ago.
We're at The Penny Farthing,
a coffee house on Toronto's
Yorkville Avenue, where the crowds
are as thick at 3 a.m. as they
are at noon. The young Canadians
who sit for hours, sipping
nothing stronger than an espresso
and listening to poets and folk
singers, belong to a new,
socially committed, sophisticated
breed, influenced by the immi-
grant tide around them, the urban
complex and the new affluence
which their parents did not
know. To see how the country has
changed, compare this photo with
earlier ones: the house-raising on
page 53, say, or the beer parlour
on page 101, or the croquet game
away back there on page 39.

IF YOUR CONSCIENCE
DEMANDS IT . . .

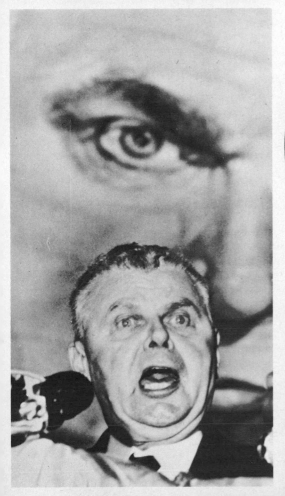

PICTURE CREDITS

49 IBC; EB.
50 NPA.
51 PA; NPA.
52 JC; PA.
53 Saskatchewan Archives.
54 SA; EB.
55 From an Ole Larsen negative in
    the Lord Beaverbrook Collection; GF.
56 J. V. Salmon Collection.
57 NPA.
58 PA; PA.
60 H. Pollard (from Miller Services); PA.
61 PA.
63 JC.
64 Ontario Archives.
66 EB.
67 EB; EB; EB.
68 The T. Eaton Co. Ltd.; NSM.
69 Bell Family and National Geographic Society;
    JC.
70 MA.
71 PA; PA.
72 JC; NPA.
73 JC; JC.
74 JC; JC.
76 EB; JC.
77 JC.
78 GF.
79 National Aviation Museum, Ottawa; PA; GF;
80 JC; NAM; NAM.
81 PA; PA; JC.
82 Manitoba Archives, from the
    L. B. Foote Collection.
85 JC.
86 Windsor Star; WS.
87 Toronto Star Syndicate; WS; WS.
88 LBF.
89 LBF; LBF; JC.
90 John Boyd Collection (from Miller Services).

91 JC.
92 The T. Eaton Co. Ltd; JC; JC.
93 JC; JC; LBF.
94 SA.
96 TS.
97 MA: SA.
98 JC; No credit; Wide World Photo
    (from Wheeler Syndicate).
99 CBC Still Photo Department; PA; TS;
    Ted Underhill.
100 National Film Board; NFB; NFB.
101 NFB; NFB; NFB.
102 NFB.
103 John de Visser.
105 John Sebert.
106 Kryn Taconis; Henri Rossier.
107 Horst Ehricht; Horst Ehricht.
108 Horst Ehricht; Capital Press.
109 John de Visser.
110 Horst Ehricht.
111 Canada Wide Photo; Don Newlands.
112 CW; Henri Rossier.
113 Don Newlands.
114 John de Visser; Henri Rossier.
115 John de Visser; John de Visser.
116 The Telegram, Toronto; CW.
117 TS; NAM; CW; CW.
118 The Globe and Mail, Toronto; CW; CW.
119 Don Newlands.
120 Horst Ehricht.
122 Horst Ehricht.
123 Don Newlands.
124 PA; PA; JB; GF; Don Newlands; Don Newlands;
    EB; EB; EB; PA; Toronto Harbour
    Commissioners; EB.
125 PA: CW: Kryn Taconis; PA; JC; CW;
    Wide World Photo; EB; Horst Ehricht;
    Horst Ehricht; Authenticated News (from
    Miller Services).
128 NPA.

Type for the text of this book is 10 point Baskerville, composed by Cooper & Beatty, Limited. It was printed in Canada on Cartier Litho paper by Litho-Print Limited. The case was printed by Sampson Matthews Limited, made by The Ryerson Press, and bound by T. H. Best Limited.